The early version of 'His Master's Voice', showing a Phonograph. Francis Barraud took this photograph before over-painting an Improved Gramophone.

OLD GRAMOPHONES
AND OTHER TALKING MACHINES

Benet Bergonzi

Shire Publications Ltd

CONTENTS

Published in 1995 by Shire Publications Ltd, Cromwell House, Church Street, Princes Risborough, Buckinghamshire HP27 9AA, UK. Copyright © 1991 by Benet Bergonzi. First published 1991; reprinted 1995. Shire Album 260. ISBN 0 7478 0104 5.

Printed in Great Britain by CIT Printing Services, Press Buildings, Merlins Bridge, Haverfordwest, Dyfed SA61 1XF.

British Library Cataloguing in Publication Data: Bergonzi, Benet. Old gramophones and other talking machines. 1. Record players, to 1925. I. Title 621. 38933. ISBN 0-7478-0104-5.

ACKNOWLEDGEMENTS
The author is indebted to Christopher Proudfoot and George Frow for a great deal of help with illustrations and text, and to Nigel Bewley and Lawrance Atkinson for assistance with photography. Illustrations are acknowledged as follows: *BBC Engineering Training Manual* (1942), page 8 (bottom); Christies South Kensington Limited, pages 4 (bottom), 11 (top left), 12 (top), 14 (top), 15, 18 (top and bottom right), 20 (left), 21 (inset), 24 (top), 27 (bottom left) and 28; Crown Copyright (Public Record Office: COPY 1/147), page 1; *Edison and His Phonograph* (J. Lewis Young, 1890; reprint), page 5 (centre); EMI Ltd, pages 18 (bottom left), 21 (bottom) and 26; George Frow, pages 5 (bottom) and 9; *The Phonograph and How to Use it* (National Phonograph Company, 1900), page 2; *The Phonograph and Phonograph-Graphophone* (New York, 1888; reprint), page 5 (top); Richard Rennie, page 30; the Trustees of the Science Museum, pages 3, 17 and 23 (top left). All other illustrations, including the cover, show objects held in the National Sound Archive and are the copyright of the British Library Board.

Cover: *The Pathéphone Modèle F of 1906 was not really a gramophone. Its discs were vertical-cut and played with a jewelled stylus, unlike conventional lateral-cut records from, say, HMV, which required frequently changed steel needles. The turntable brake release is above the decal in the foreground. The horn is of the popular 'Morning Glory' type.*

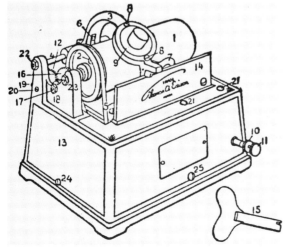

This index of parts, printed in 1900, shows the main components of a typical small phonograph (horn removed). Parts discussed in this book include the mandrel (1), the speaker or reproducer (9) and the feedscrew (hidden behind the mandrel). The cast iron case conceals the spring-driven motor.

621.389   BER

Checked

17/9/11

Hertfordshire
COUNTY COUNCIL

Community Information

14 FEB 2001

9/12

Edison's tinfoil Phonograph of 1877, the first ever machine for recording and reproducing sound. There are two diaphragm/stylus assemblies: the one facing us is the recorder, the other the reproducer. The feedscrew, by which the foil-covered mandrel moved past the stylus while recording, was to change little on later machines, though more often the recorder/reproducer was to move.

THE PHONOGRAPH

In 1877 the young American scientist Thomas Edison was working on automatic repeaters for telegraph messages in Morse code. While investigating the cutting of dots and dashes into a wax-covered tablet, he realised it would be possible to indent in the wax vibrations of his speech via a stylus attached to the centre of a diaphragm. After trying to indent the vibrations in a spiral on a flat disc, Edison decided a cylinder was mechanically better. A metal cylinder with a light spiral guide-groove was covered with a layer of tinfoil. As the stylus vibrated, the foil was indented along the course of the guide-groove. Edison's Phonograph was patented in 1878, and a few examples were produced for sale. British copies can still be collected today. The tinfoil phonograph had many shortcomings: foils were easily damaged, could not be listened to easily and were impossible to copy. By 1879 Edison had turned his attentions elsewhere.

In 1886, in Washington DC, Charles Sumner Tainter and Chichester Bell, cousin of A. G. Bell, inventor of the telephone, patented an improved phonograph called the Graphophone. Its recordings were superior because the stylus could cut into wax rather than indented foil. The wax covered the surface of interchangeable cardboard cylinders measuring 6 inches (15.5 cm) long by 1¼ inches (3 cm) in diameter. Challenged by the Graphophone, Edison produced, in 1888, the Perfected Phonograph. It used all-wax cylinders, 4 by 2¼ inches (10 by 5.7 cm), lasting approximately two minutes. The recorder and reproducer were mounted on a 'spectacle' carrier arm for easy interchangeability. Motive power for Phonograph and Graphophone was either by treadle (as in a sewing machine) or electric motor, using cumbersome wet-cell batteries.

The two instruments were marketed solely for dictation, being rented out to offices. The United States was divided

3

Thomas Edison with the Perfected Phonograph, 1888. This photograph is said to have been taken at 5 am after a 72-hour crash programme of work to iron out problems before the phonograph was put into production. Edison is using rubber hearing tubes which had to be inserted right into the ear. It is ironic that he suffered from deafness.

The original Bell-Tainter Graphophone played long, narrow wax-covered cylinders. Its advantage in comparison with the Edison Phonograph of 1888 was that the cylinders' design made it easy to find a passage in a dictation, but, on the other hand, recordings could not be 'shaved' off to allow reuse. This late (1893-4) model has an electric motor and detachable mandrel for Edison-sized cylinders.

Above: *The Phonograph and Graphophone were initially marketed exclusively as office dictation machines, for rental only. Neither achieved success. These pictures date from 1888; at that time the typewriter itself was a novelty in many offices. Stenographers' opposition to the threat to their jobs was to be well organised, particularly in Britain.*

Below: *This diagram from a book of 1890 illustrates the principle of cylinder recording. At first the 'holes' (top row) encapsulating the sound were dents in tinfoil, before they became sharper incisions in wax.*

into territories by a number of companies under a single holding company. There was little thought of making pre-recorded musical recordings. The Phonograph was more popular than the Graphophone (by 1891, of four hundred machines on rental in Washington, only fifteen were Graphophones), but neither achieved the great success hoped for. During the early 1890s the companies turned to the more profitable line of music. Arcades for coin-in-slot phonographs sprang up, and people queued to hear even crude recordings of popular songs, listening through hearing tubes poked into the ears. Although showmen could make large profits, the quality from the individually cut cylinders was poor.

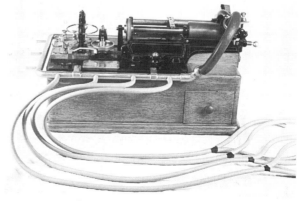

Right: *The first entertainment recordings were played on phonographs like this electrically driven Edison Class M of the mid-1890s. Exhibitors could make a handsome profit, with twelve people paying to listen to a single cylinder via the 'gallery' from the reproducer and multiple ear-tubes.*

Above: *Original versions of three well-known Edison Phonographs. The Home (right) has the bulky layout typical of early Edisons and dates from 1896-1901. The Standard (left), most popular of all phonographs, was made in this style between 1898 and 1900. The Gem (1899-1900) was cheapest and was initially sold uncased. With many variations, these models remained in production until 1913.*

Left: *Kämmer und Reinhardt Gramophone, about 1895. The earliest mass-produced Gramophones were cheap and crude compared with contemporary phonographs. The horn on this example, which is preserved at the National Sound Archive, is a modern replica.*

Right: *Only with the introduction of the spring motor did the Gramophone achieve popularity. This is a later (1901) version of the Improved Gramophone developed in 1896, and known as the 'Trademark' after it featured in the 'His Master's Voice' painting.*

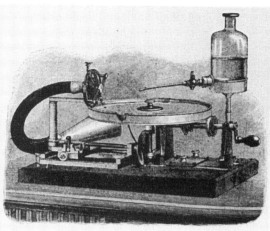

Left: *Emile Berliner (1851-1929)*.

Right: *Berliner's recording machine, 1888. The horn at the end of the flexible tube collected sound so that, at the other end, vibrations would strike the diaphragm attached to a stylus, which cut a wavy groove in the wax disc. The bottle contained alcohol, to stop dust from adhering to the stylus.*

THE GRAMOPHONE

In 1888 the German-American Emile Berliner (1851-1929) demonstrated a new type of talking machine. While Edison had conceived of recording on discs, the novelty of Berliner's invention was that the movements of the cutting stylus in sympathy with the diaphragm were lateral but flat, from one side of the groove to the other, rather than vertical, or 'hill and dale', as on the Phonograph. The stylus cut through an even layer of wax spread on a zinc base. Then the disc was immersed in acid, which ate into the metal, cutting a deeper groove between the areas still protected by wax. The zinc master record could be used to make a metal matrix with a ridge instead of a groove and this was used for pressing as many as five hundred or one thousand copies of the recording in a suitable thermoplastic. Pressings had a loud, deep groove, and this meant the playback instrument, or Gramophone, needed no feedscrew, its stylus being propelled across the record simply because it followed the groove, and thus it could be made more cheaply than a Phonograph or Graphophone. The domestic user could not record his or her own gramophone records, as was possible with a phonograph.

In 1889 Berliner revisited Germany to demonstrate his invention and contracted a firm of toymakers in Waltershausen, Kämmer und Reinhardt, to produce the first Gramophones. The rudimentary hand-powered instruments were produced with slight variations from 1889 to the mid 1890s. Many were imported to Britain. The discs were 5 inches (12.5 cm) in diameter. They were made of celluloid or vulcanite (hard rubber) and are thought to have been pressed at a plant in Mannheim where dolls' heads were made. The speed of the records varied from 90 to 110 revolutions per minute (rpm) and can be established today only by trial and error. None lasted more than one minute. Sound was louder than from cylinders, but no better.

During the early 1890s Berliner set up his own company in the USA. There, 7 inch (18 cm) vulcanite records were produced, running at 70 rpm and, from 1894 onwards, unlike the German records, recorded by professional artists.

An economy version of the Improved Gramophone marketed in 1901, the Style 3 dispensed with the wooden casing to reveal Eldridge Johnson's simple and reliable motor.

Apart from a few with electric motors, the larger American gramophones were still driven manually, and thus not very popular. In 1896 the Improved Gramophone appeared, to immediate success. It was powered by a reliable spring motor built and designed by a New Jersey mechanical engineer, Eldridge R. Johnson. The following year Johnson designed an improved soundbox (the stylus/diaphragm assembly). Recording for the Gramophone was comparatively attractive to singers and other artists because several copies could be produced from one good wax and they were less likely to have to perform the same piece repeatedly, a common feature of cylinder recording. Hence Berliner's recording expert, Fred Gaisberg, could sign up popular opera singers.

In 1898 a London branch of Berliner's business, called the Gramophone Company, opened a cramped office in a Covent Garden basement. At first all instruments (in component form) and discs were shipped from the United States, but within a few months Gaisberg arrived to start recording, and a record-pressing plant opened. For fear of trouble from a union-organised British workforce, the plant was in Germany, combined with the existing Hanover telephone factory of Emile Berliner's brother

Joseph, although the offices and studio were in London. In 1899 the Gramophone Company purchased what is probably the world's most famous trademark, Francis Barraud's 'His Master's Voice', showing an Improved Gramophone. Nipper the terrier had originally been depicted listening to a phonograph, but this was altered at the Gramophone Company's request.

In 1900 Gramophone record quality was greatly improved when zinc masters were replaced by solid wax recording blanks. After the groove had been cut, they were covered with graphite powder, which enabled them to be electroplated, and it was from this plating, when detached, that a better stamper could be derived. While the soft wax of cylinders required a delicate jewel stylus for reproduction, discs, being made of tougher material, could be played with a steel needle. In the early days even old sewing needles were recommended! The vulcanite rubber compound was coarse and tended to warp when cooling in the factory. Fred Gaisberg found a better material at a button factory in Newark, New Jersey. The patent button composition containing shellac (a resin derived from the secretion of the beetle *Coccus lacca* found in Malaya), with the addition of powdered slate, altered little until the end of 78 rpm records in the 1950s. The slate was to sharpen the needles as they played, ensuring a good fit to the record's unique groove; hence it became essential to change needles frequently.

The principle of disc recording. The groove's wavelength varies with the sound's frequency, shown here in cycles per second.

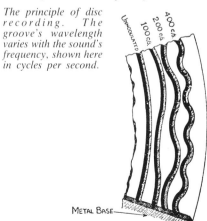

8

The first successful spring motor put into production was designed by J. E. Greenhill of London. Made of heavy brass, a few examples were sold during the mid 1890s, in their own cases for attachment to previously electric Phonographs.

CYLINDER VERSUS DISC

Following the development of the Perfected Phonograph in the United States a British company, Edison Bell, was formed to hire out Phonographs and Bell-Tainter Graphophones. As in America, it was found that the former were more popular. In 1893 Edison began supplying a special Phonograph to Edison Bell: produced in three versions, the Commercial, Exhibition and Domestic, all electrically driven from batteries, it was available for hire only, and the hirer had to sign strict agreements governing its use. Other companies were illicitly importing Edison instruments and pre-recorded cylinders. To ensure only Edison Bell's officially sanctioned pre-recorded product could be replayed, for a short time feedscrew and cylinders were threaded at 200 threads per inch (2.5 cm) instead of the standard 100 tpi. One of these instruments featured in the original 'His Master's Voice' painting.

While efficient, the wet batteries were messy and had a limited life. In 1891 the Englishman J. E. Greenhill demonstrated to Edison's London representative, George Gouraud, a clockwork motor he had invented for the Phonograph, and a few were manufactured for sale to Phonograph owners, but it was not until 1896 that Edison's first Phonograph with a spring motor was marketed. Designed in America by Frank Capps, the motor replaced Greenhill's fan-governor with a fly-ball weight governor and was fitted underneath the feedscrew/mandrel assembly. The motor of the 'Spring Motor Phonograph' had three springs, each giving up the same amount of energy in sequence so that up to fourteen cylinders could be played for each winding. Smaller versions soon followed: the durable Home, Standard and Gem models.

A spring-motored Graphophone was then already available. In 1894 the Columbia Phonograph Company General (partly based on a small concern which had rented out dictation machines in the Washington area) became holder of the Bell-Tainter patents and brought out a new Graphophone designed by the Scotsman Thomas Macdonald. It used a tapered mandrel for solid wax cylinders of the Edison size cut at 100 threads per inch and was powered by a compact single-spring motor. While Macdonald's design infringed several Edison patents, his company's riposte to Edison was that under the Bell-Tainter patents only they had the right to record in wax. A long-running legal dispute resulted. The new Graphophone was a popular home entertainment instrument. In 1897 Columbia opened a European headquarters in Paris, and in 1900 it transferred to London. By the turn of the century all normal-sized cylinders were standardised at 100 threads per inch and 160 rpm, giving two minutes' playing time.

When the Gramophone Company was established, Edison Bell was the main British talking-machine company, offering imported and (after 1904) British-made phonographs. Soon after 'His Master's Voice' was painted, Eldridge R. Johnson, manufacturing gramophones for the British market but selling none in the USA owing to a legal dispute with Berliner, started a new company of his own, calling the gramophones 'Victors' and immediately arranging to adopt the British trademark. Victors (the name continued after Johnson reached agreement with Berliner) were practically indistinguishable from British Gramophones, and this was to continue even after 1918, when the gramophones were finally 100 per cent British-made.

Edison's first commercial moulded cylinders were put on sale in the United States in December 1901, and two years later similar cylinders were being produced at the Edison Bell factory in Peckham, south London. It had taken time for the companies to arrive at a reliable process for electroplating a wax master cylinder so that a mould could be 'grown' from it, and then to find a suitable thermoplastic wax compound which would shrink cleanly on cooling for safe withdrawal from the mould. By this time gramophone records were longer and louder and rapidly gaining in popularity. In 1902 Columbia's gramophone competitor, the very similar Disc Graphophone, was launched in the USA.

On the European mainland, talking-machine manufacturers were proliferating. The largest was the French company Pathé Frères, which initially made a phonograph based on the Columbia Graphophone. Also from France was

By spring 1896 Edison Spring Motor Phonographs were being offered with motors designed by Frank Capps of the United States Phonograph Company. Edison purchased this company, and the motors continued with little alteration for many years. The three-spring mechanism seems over-engineered by later standards, but multi-cylinder playing was needed to compete with electric motors. In these two views of the same machine, the prop is not original, but the oil-can is.

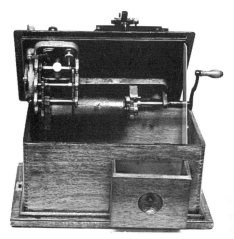 

Left: *Type N Graphophone, 1895. One of the earliest spring-motored models, it was the first to have a fixed mandrel for Edison-style cylinders, acknowledging the failure of the Bell-Tainter design. However, mechanically the N was briefly in advance of any Edison product. While rare today, it resembles more common later Graphophones.*

Right: *The 'His Master's Voice' Phonograph, made by Edison for the British market (Edison Bell), was similar to this 'Commercial' version of about 1895. It has a speaking tube and typewriter-style stop and start keys. Unlike contemporary American Edisons, the feedscrew is not in line with the mandrel but behind it. The original glass battery has never been used.*

Below: *Type B Graphophone: an example dating from about 1900 of a model introduced in 1897. The B was nicknamed 'Eagle' — slang for its 10 dollars selling price. The smallest and cheapest of phonographs when introduced, the Eagle was produced by the thousand and there were many imitators.*

Henri Lioret, whose company pioneered celluloid-moulded cylinders and even tried some four-minute cylinders. One of Lioret's phonographs was virtually pocket-sized. His cylinders were incompatible with those of other makers, and the company failed. Pathé was successful, selling a wide range of phonographs. Many German manufacturers produced cheap machines sold in Britain under various names, which brought recorded sound within reach of many. The Puck,

Thorens Royal, about 1904-7. Though normally unlabelled, a Thorens can be recognised by its arched motor plates and lyre-shaped end support. It is based on the 'Eagle' Graphophone. Most of the working parts are nickel-plated. The aluminium horn is a modern replica.

The Lioret No. 2 and Le Merveilleux portable phonographs, of about 1900. The clockmaker Henri Lioret of Paris produced unique phonographs to play his patent celluloid cylinders, each on an integral brass mandrel, its strong groove allowing the phonograph's normal feedscrew to be dispensed with. The large cardboard reproducer gives loud sound despite the flimsiness of the celluloid 'horn'. The internal-horn Merveilleux is one of the smallest of all phonographs, just 8 inches (20 cm) high. It played only cylinders lasting thirty seconds.

Puck Phonograph (right) and Kastenpuck, about 1903. Cheap German phonographs without feedscrews were often known generically as 'Pucks' even if produced by other makers. Typically, the cast iron base is lyre-shaped. The Kastenpuck (a proprietary term) appears to have a cabinet but it is only a pedestal since all the working parts are on top. Without a feedscrew, wax cylinders were difficult to play, especially when worn.

13

(Left) A Kämmer und Reinhardt gramophone with original horn, about 1894. (Centre) A 1908 New Melba, a Gramophone Company de luxe model, one of the last with a metal 'Morning Glory' horn before laminated wood was adopted in the upper price range. (Right) An entirely plated Nickel King from Symphonion of Leipzig, with inferior parallel-bore tone arm.

The Gramophone Company loaned a top-of-the-range Monarch with wooden horn to Captain Scott's last expedition, 1910-13. This photograph was taken in Antarctica in 1911.

Above left: *Columbia BD (Majestic) Disc Graphophone, about 1910. From 1905 Columbia disc instruments had been available with tone arms, unlike those of Gramophones, pivoting vertically as well as laterally at the horn end. The expensive Majestic differed from earlier Columbias in its sleek, minimally decorated appearance. The horn resembles a 'Morning Glory' but is of one-piece construction.*

Above right: *The Symphony Victory, about 1910, was put together by a small company, possibly the east London factor Blankenstein. The soundbox, tone arm and back bracket are by the Gramophone Company subsidiary Zonophone and date from about 1905. Other components may be by Symphonion of Germany. Such assembled gramophones are often found.*

Right: *The later version of the Johnson motor had a barrel-enclosed mainspring and a diagonally mounted governor linked to the speed adjuster near the turntable, and it was easily accessible via a hinged motor board. The patent Victor/Gramophone Company tone arm shows the 'gooseneck' end pivoted upwards to support the soundbox. The motor shown is one of the last made before the re-design of 1905.*

15

for instance, cost just 3s 6d — the price of two or three cylinders. Switzerland also became a manufacturing centre: one maker's name, Thorens, survives today on hi-fi equipment. None of the cylinder makers could compete with the discs' musical repertoire. For greater playing time, in 1901 10 inch (25 cm) discs had been introduced. The first Gramophone to play them was called the Monarch; a modified 'Trademark' instrument was also offered.

In 1903 12 inch (30 cm) discs arrived, and the tone arm was introduced by Victor/Gramophone. This was a pivoted metal tube between the soundbox and horn, hinged to travel across the record. Its technical importance was that the whole horn no longer had to move and could therefore be made heavier and better. In 1904 the 'Morning Glory' horn first appeared, its 'petals' made of steel or brass. Four years later buyers were given the option of softer-toned laminated wood horns. Motors were improved as well. Models after the Trademark had barrel-enclosed mainsprings so the handle no longer turned anti-clockwise as the record played and could be wound up during playing. In 1905 a new simpler motor was offered, the first to drive the turntable direct from the spring-barrel, via an endless screw on the spindle. These developments were originated by Victor in the USA. After about 1905 the gramophone improved little acoustically for the next twenty years. In 1907 the huge Columbia company abandoned sales of cylinders and phonographs, throwing all its resources behind the ever more popular disc. Significantly, in the same year the Gramophone Company opened a British record factory at Hayes, west of London.

Senior Monarch Gramophone on pedestal, about 1904-5; the most expensive of the Monarch range, with triple-spring motor, patented tapered tone arm and 12 inch (30 cm) turntable. The black metal horn has a brass mouth. The optional pedestal is purely for storage.

A later version of the 1904 Holzweissig Hymnophon whose concealed horn may have inspired the first internal-horn gramophone made by Victor the following year.

UNUSUAL TALKING MACHINES

Cylinder records were made using a phonograph similar to a consumer model but with a different stylus/diaphragm, whereas disc records required a special gramophone equipped with a feedscrew to cut the spiral groove. In the Gramophone Company's version the cutting head and recording horn were stationary; the turntable moved laterally while revolving. Early recording experts became skilled at getting the best out of their insensitive equipment. Stringed instruments were too quiet to record well as part of an orchestra. The problem was solved by a hybridisation of violin-family instruments with talking machines themselves. The inventor, Charles Stroh, replaced the wooden body and bridge with a diaphragm and metal horn to amplify better.

In 1904 the German maker Holzweissig produced a new gramophone, the Hymnophon, whose horn curved down from the tone arm rather than up and was fed through the case under the turntable, only its mouth being visible at the front. Possibly based on this, the internal-horn Victor Victrola appeared in 1906. In a large floor-standing cabinet giving ample storage space for records, it proved immediately popular, despite its high price (the British version was launched at £60 in 1907) and the surprising fact that the internal horn when introduced was a retrograde step acoustically. Its boxy shape and cast iron throat distorted or deadened many sound frequencies: the only advantage was that with the lid shut the needle's 'scratch' in the groove was not heard. Other makers rushed to produce copies. Columbia's Grafonola was available in cabinets disguised as pianos or desks. By 1910 the Glasgow dealer Murdoch could advertise ten internal-horn machines out of a total range of 45 makes of disc instrument. The same year

17

the Gramophone Company lost its legal attempts to retain 'gramophone' as a proprietary term. All other companies operating in Britain began using the word. The original company increasingly adopted the trading name 'His Master's Voice'. In the USA the word 'gramophone' had fallen into disuse: they were known either as Victors or generically as (disc) phonographs.

Edison Bell's first disc instrument, the Discaphone, appeared in 1908. The same year, Edison in the United States solved the problem of the comparatively short playing time of cylinders, launching the new 200 threads per inch, four-minute Amberol cylinders, which bettered even 12 inch discs. They could be played on

Above: *Stollwerck Toy Gramophone, about 1903. The cheap tinplate (shown) or wooden machine played only its own 3½ inch (9 cm) discs, which were often made of chocolate though more conventional material was also used. Stollwercks are very rare today.*

Below left: *A Gramophone Company disc lathe. Quite distinct from the domestic gramophone, its soundbox is mounted on a bridge under which the turntable traversed while revolving, so that an even groove would be cut in the wax blank. Motive power was by a falling-weight system. The recording horn is missing.*

Below right: *The inventor Charles Stroh amplified stringed instruments by connecting the bridge to the centre of a diaphragm with a horn on its other side. There was no need for a conventional body. Many Stroh instruments were made and can often be found today. This is a cello.*

Left: *The Grand was the Gramophone Company's expensive version of the internal-horn Victrola. The Sheraton-style cabinet shown was 4 feet (122 cm) high. The fake drawers concealed doors to the horn. An example is preserved in the National Sound Archive.*

Right: *Edison Amberola Model I (A), about 1910. The Amberola as introduced in late 1909 had a fixed papier-mâché horn and traversing mandrel. This model's convertible reproducer and adjustable gearing play either two- or four-minute cylinders. The drawers below the fretwork grille can store up to one hundred cylinders. The metal parts are decorated by deliberate oxidisation.*

almost any Edison phonograph, given a new reproducer and adjusted gearing. Unfortunately for sales, the musical repertoire was inferior to the gramophone's. Edison's reply to the Victrola was the expensive internal-horn Amberola phonograph, initially in a massive and complex cabinet including drawers with individual cylinder compartments. In 1912 the greatly improved 'Blue Amberol' was announced. Cast in celluloid and produced in the USA for worldwide distribution, it marked the apex of cylinder sound reproduction. Edison's last domestic external-horn phonograph was the Opera of 1911-13. Because of the

hardness of the new cylinders it could use a diamond stylus. As with the tinfoil phonograph, the cylinder traversed past a fixed reproducer while playing. This enabled the fine wood 'Music Master' horn to be self-supporting, obviating the need for the previous swivelling attachment to a horn-crane. Other makers, such as Columbia, had solved the problem by fitting a gramophone-style tone arm.

Even playing hard synthetic records, acoustic instruments could not produce enough sound for some applications. One early attempt to augment the horn was the Auxetophone, invented by the Englishman Charles Parsons. An electric

Left: *The Gramophone Model XIV of 1911 put the Grand's boxy horn into a new lavish cabinet based on the vaguely 'Louis XV' Victrola of 1909. This style for luxury models continued from both companies until the mid 1920s and was copied by other makers. Some later examples have serpentine fronts and sides.*

Right: *Primaphone, about 1912: a later example of the model introduced by Edison Bell in 1909. Its distinctive features — a folding horn compromising between internal and external, and a fixed but telescopic tone arm evading the Gramophone Company's patent on tapered arms — were patented by J. M. Landon of south London.*

compressor in the cabinet created a flow of air to be modulated in the soundbox and emerge from the horn. As well as its intended application for large concerts, an Auxetophone was used on occasion in the recording studio for crude horn-to-horn 'mixing'. In 1906 Pathé, one of Europe's largest manufacturers, abandoned phonograph production and introduced a new design of disc instrument. The discs were vertical-cut: as in cylinders, the modulations within the groove were cut downwards. They played only on the new Pathéphone disc instruments with jewelled styli, although kits to adapt conventional gramophones became available later. Pathéphones can be distinguished from gramophones by the fact that the soundbox's large diaphragm is at right-angles to the tone arm. Discs started at the centre and played towards the edge.

In 1912 Edison at last re-adopted the disc. His version too was vertical-cut and

Left: *HMV Model VIII. An example of about 1913 of the oak-cased version of HMV's first table grand introduced in 1910. Table grands were a durable design from all manufacturers. The VIII's internal horn was crude, with the motor inside it just behind the grille. Its price, £12 10s, compares with £50 for the XIV or £6 to £7 for a better sounding external-horn instrument.*

Below: *Sir Charles Parsons first demonstrated his Auxetophone in 1904, and from 1906 the Gramophone Company marketed the instrument at £100. The compressor cabinet was the size of many internal-horn gramophones. Despite the Auxetophone's suitability for open-air concerts, its compressor needed an electricity supply.*

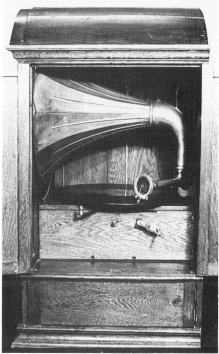

Left: Edison Opera, 1912. The Opera, renamed Concert in 1912, was the open-horn counterpart to the early Amberola. Beautifully made (this example is mahogany), it gave possibly the best sound of any contemporary instrument, cylinder or disc.

Right: In 1906 Pathé Frères abandoned production of phonographs in favour of their own vertical-cut centre-start disc instruments. The Majestic of 1909 enclosed its 'Morning Glory' horn in a massive cabinet. It could play 20 inch (51 cm) discs. Running at 120 rpm, they played no longer than Pathé's standard discs but were louder.

did not replace the Amberol cylinders (two-minute cylinders had been discontinued) but was sold alongside them. Incompatible with any other instrument but Edison's Disc Phonograph, the 10 inch (25 cm) discs had 150 grooves per inch (finer than the Pathés') and played for four to five minutes. They were moulded in condensite, an advanced phenolic plastic varnished, before moulding, on to a thick shellac core. The Disc Phonographs were available in a wide range of internal-horn cabinets, many modelled on classical period furniture. Working parts varied little. The tone arm was rigid between reproducer and horn, so that the horn swivelled round as the record played, driven by a rack mechanism analogous to the cylinder machines' feedscrew. Following a fire at Edison's New Jersey factory, and the outbreak of the First World War, sales were difficult. The war was over before marketing of the highly priced discs and instruments began in Britain. By now the Amberola was the only cylinder phonograph still being made anywhere in the world. The Disc Phonograph did nothing to increase the dwindling band of loyal Edison supporters. The gramophone had won the popularity battle.

Early gramophones such as the Trademark were small and light and could easily be carried about in optional leather

Above left: *The Decca portable was introduced in 1914 by the long-established London musical-instrument makers Barnett Samuel. The Decca record company was not set up until 1929. This bullet-holed example is one of many to have seen service during the First World War.*

Above right: *The mid 1920s Edison Bell Picturegram, an internal-horn portable whose 'horn' was the well beside the turntable, provided visual aids — a paper roll of pictures accompanied the fairy stories on record. Drive was by a crude friction wheel on the turntable rim. The awkward system was not popular.*

Below left: *Edison Disc Phonograph Chalet Model, about 1919. Although approximately 20 inches (51 cm) cubed, the 'table grand' Chalet was one of the smallest and cheapest of Edison Disc Phonographs. Its price in Britain, £40 (1921), was still too high for popularity. The fretwork grille is missing, revealing the swivelling horn.*

Below right: *The World Record Controller, sold from 1922 to about 1926. A rubber-tyred friction wheel was used on the disc's surface to ensure that the linear speed of the stylus in the groove was constant; a conventional governor was used to brake the friction wheel so it applied drag to the turntable at the start of the record, which progressively eased as the controller moved towards the centre. This gramophone is slightly later.*

carrying cases. This became difficult later as turntables and horns grew larger. Several companies produced portable gramophones, often using small internal horns. Much the most successful early portable came from the old-established London firm of Barnett Samuel. Their Decca, launched on the eve of the First World War, employed an ingenious external horn amplifying sound via a reflector in the lid of the briefcase-like cabinet. Sound quality was considered excellent: the Decca was popular with troops in the trenches and continued to sell widely well into the 1920s.

In the post-war years many more portables were offered. None was quite so odd as the Flamephone, which, for uncertain scientific reasons, substituted a gas jet above the soundbox for a horn of any sort. In 1922 the World Record Controller was offered by its inventor, Noel Pemberton-Billing. This was an accessory for any gramophone which, by means of a feedscrew and governor, modified the turntable speed to give an effective constant 'linear speed' (the speed of the stylus in the groove), as with a phonograph. The Controller could only be used when playing special World records. Although it bravely attempted to solve a problem basic to disc recording, poor repertoire and high prices led to the system's failure.

Above: In 1925 HMV launched the short-lived models 510 (shown) and 460 based on the Lumière brothers' earlier patent for a 'soundbox' with a pleated diaphragm, so large that no horn was needed. Conventional horn developments soon made the models obsolete, though some of their cabinets were rebuilt for internal horns.

Right: The Gramophone Style Number 6 of 1901, a slightly enlarged Trademark model, could easily be transported in its leather case.

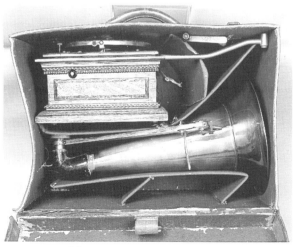

Peter Pan 'box camera' portables. The original version of 1922 (right) had a telescopic aluminium horn, while the Improved Peter Pan of 1924 used a conventional tone arm leading to a folding leather horn in the open lid. The turntables are made up of four arms.

THE LAST ACOUSTICS

Phonographs and gramophones using horns for amplification date from a period when the differences between rich and poor were great. A large proportion of the instruments left to us now, with hand-finished oak or mahogany cabinets, would have cost the equivalent of thousands of pounds today. Many more popularly priced machines were sold, but they were cheaply made and are less likely to have been preserved.

The outbreak of the First World War had immediately ended supplies of cheap German components and instruments into Britain and, munitions work and steel shortages permitting, new firms sprang up to fill the gap. In the early 1920s some companies that were for a long time household names were established: Collaro, Garrard and Alba, for example. Proprietary components became available for home assemblers to build their own gramophones or update old ones. Such 'mongrel' instruments are often found today, the woodwork by amateur cabinet-makers. Miniature portables were developed for walkers and cyclists. The ingenious folding Peter Pan

and Cameraphone were bulky compared with the truly pocket-sized Swiss-made Mikiphone, launched in Britain in 1926. The more expensive cabinets remained as lavish as ever. Electric motors returned for the first time since the wet-battery era, as by now the wealthy might be expected to have mains power. In Britain, as elsewhere, the gramophone was not only growing in popularity but increasingly being accepted by serious music lovers: the magazine *The Gramophone* was founded in 1923 by the writer Compton Mackenzie.

In 1925 the microphone, used for many years in telephone and radio, was at last developed for recording. Victor, Columbia and HMV issued the first discs recorded using the new Western Electric process. Other companies quickly followed. A new type of Victrola, still using an acoustic internal horn, was designed for the new records. So that it would fit internally, the exponentially tapering horn divided at two points into two sections, the four conduits re-uniting at the mouth, which filled the whole front of the cabinet. It was two years before the

Below right: *Cutaway model of a Re-entrant horn, used in such HMVs as the 203 (shown overleaf), looking into the horn from the front to show its complex construction. The horns were made of terneplate (lead-plated steel.)*

British version of the 'Orthophonic Victrola' was available, Victor's sister HMV introducing the electric records with a new, but less sophisticated, design of internal folded horn.

Older-style gramophones were still available, HMV even launching a new open-horn model, the 32 (HMV's last) in 1927. It cost just £9, compared with over £70 for the new 'Re-entrant' horn models. The true enthusiast could buy uncompromising 'Handmade Gramophones' from the British maker E. M. Ginn, under the name of 'EMG' and later 'Expert'. These had external horns of exponential taper, the diameters of whose mouths were often as large as 33½ inches (85 cm)! Ginn's instruments were made from the late 1920s until the 1940s. HMV's rivals boasted scientific-sounding names for their new internal-horn instruments such as Columbia's 'Viva Tonal' and Lockwood's 'Micro-Perophone Chromogram'.

Above: *The Swiss-made Mikiphone, probably the smallest gramophone ever placed on the market, folded up to the size of a large pocket watch. Records of up to 10 inches (25 cm) could be played, the design relying on the rigidity of shellac since the turntable was far smaller than the disc.*

Below left: *During the early 1920s expensive gramophones became grander. The Aeolian Vocalion in a Chinese Chippendale-style cabinet was 4 feet 8 inches (1.42 metres) high, with (not shown) a cable-operated remote volume mute, and storage as well as the horn behind the front grille.*

Below right: *Columbia (British) Model 153 Console Grafonola, about 1927. The console type of gramophone was bulky compared to the size of its horn. The louvres to the horn aperture are a Columbia characteristic. The Viva Tonal horn was bifurcated like its HMV rival, but Columbia's instrument cost only about one-third of the price.*

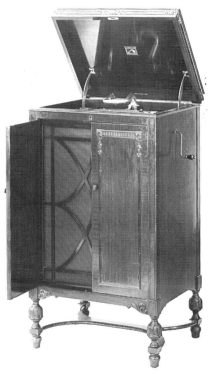

the long-players were acoustically cut. With the Depression looming, in October 1929 the Edison domestic phonograph and record factories were closed down, leaving only his office dictation business.

Electrical reproduction was now replacing the horn. Development of the valve amplifier led to electric loudspeakers, giving sound that was louder than before, and adjustable. Although all-electric gramophones originated as early as 1925 in the USA with the very expensive Brunswick Panatrope, radio's popularity was such that electric reproduction of records generally started via the radio's loudspeaker, either by a new pick-up conversion kit for the wind-up gramophone, or by a speakerless 'record player' attached by a lead to the radio. Soon all was combined in the radio-gramophone. HMV's first radiogram appeared in 1929, immediately making obsolete Re-entrant horn instruments introduced only one or two years previously. Because the electric machines

Below: *Expert Senior hand-made gramophone, 1930s. From soundbox to horn mouth (dented on this example) the sound conduit tapers at a calculated rate to give better reproduction than much electrical equipment of the period.*

Above: *Most expensive of the range of Re-entrant horn HMVs introduced in 1927 was the Model 203, priced at £75 and over 4 feet (238 cm) high when closed. Its mahogany cabinet was the only difference from the cheaper oak Model 202. This 1930 example was sold in April 1990 for £6050, then a record auction price for a gramophone.*

Edison's last innovation came in 1926 — long-playing records. At a dense 450 grooves per inch (much tighter than a modern vinyl LP) the 12 inch (30 cm) discs, still vertical-cut, carried up to twenty minutes of sound per side at 80 rpm. An existing Disc Phonograph could be used if given a new reproducer and adapted mechanically. The records and adapted phonographs are rare outside the USA. Again, poor repertoire spoilt the new system's chances, as few long unbroken pieces of music, long sought by listeners, were offered. It was 1927 before Edison issued electrically recorded discs in the United States: all but one of

Above left: *Edison Amberola 50, 1915-29. In 1915 the Amberola range was simplified to three models, which reverted to travelling-reproducer design. The table model 50 was in the middle of the range. Its mahogany case is less lavish than that of earlier types.*

Above right: *HMV Model 501 Radiogram, 1931. This radiogram's walnut cabinet and fretwork speaker grille recall an acoustic instrument. Many of its competitors were more cheaply made.*

Below left: *HMV's Model 102 portable was the most durable acoustic gramophone of all, available with few changes from 1931 to 1958. The 'rim' round the turntable is a removable record container.*

Below right: *HMV Model 113a 'Transportable'. Made in Calcutta in 1941, it was one of the last spring-wound table models.*

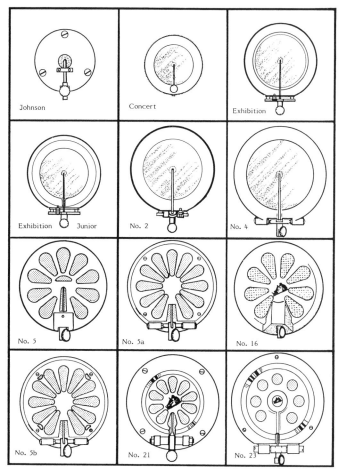

Gramophone Company soundboxes from 1897 to the last acoustics. The last six, with aluminium diaphragms rather than mica, have perforated bright metal shields. Common ones include the Johnson or 'Clark-Johnson' (1897-1903), the Exhibition (1903-1920s), the Number 4 (1925-31) and the 5a (1927 to 1930s).

were initially highly priced, acoustic reproduction persisted for a while, but, with the spread of mains electricity, by the late 1930s it was increasingly regarded as being out of date. However, portables changed little from the 1920s to the 1950s. Countries without electricity still needed acoustic instruments — HMV's Calcutta factory produced them into the 1940s. E. M. Ginn's gramophones for

purists were the last real development in acoustic reproduction quality.

Thomas Edison died in October 1931, at the age of 84. In the same year another household name originated, when in Britain the Gramophone Company (HMV) merged with its long-standing rival Columbia, to form Electric and Musical Industries (EMI).

OLD TALKING MACHINES TODAY

While museums preserve many good collections, there is still an active market in machines for sale. During the 1970s and 1980s values rose steadily, particularly for well known makes. Other instruments can be bought more cheaply, particularly if not in the best condition. Many spare parts, originals or reproductions, can be located through the City of London Phonograph and Gramophone Society, as can skilled repairers.

Gramophone records (even those dating from as long ago as 1910-20) can still be picked up in junk shops for a few pence, but dating them is a complex matter, needing a book to itself. Many specific discs are more valuable. Cylinders are less common than discs but can still be readily bought. What appears to be a light layer of mould may have ruined wax cylinders.

A range of modern re-recorded two-minute cylinders has been produced. Jewelled styli can be inspected for wear (perceptible flattened-off areas) with a 10× magnifying glass. Replacement styli are available. Edison styli should be 0.008 inch (0.2 mm) tip radius for two-minute cylinders, and 0.0047 inch (0.12 mm) for four-minute cylinders. An incorrect or worn stylus will always damage wax cylinders.

Steel needles should *never* be used on cylinders or vertical-cut discs (most likely to be Pathé or Edison). When used for gramophone records, they must be discarded after one playing of one side. New steel needles are available. Old needles labelled on the tin as suitable for playing ten records were intended only for light-weight electrical pick-ups, not acoustic soundboxes. Fibre needles are kinder to records but rarer today. When playing, the soundbox should be adjusted so that the needle is at an angle of 60 degrees to the disc surface.

All bearings and gears should be regularly lubricated on playing instruments. Most light oils are suitable. Barrel-enclosed mainsprings were lubricated with graphite grease which may have solidified after long disuse but otherwise should not need replenishment unless the barrel has been opened, for example to replace a broken spring. New springs and grease are still produced.

FURTHER READING

Andrews, Frank. *The Edison Phonograph — The British Connection.* City of London Phonograph and Gramophone Society, 1986.

Baumbach, Robert. *Look for the Dog: An Illustrated Guide to Victor Talking Machines.* Stationery X-Press (USA), 1981.

Bayley, Ernie. *The EMI Collection.* Bayley, 1977.

Chew, V. K. *Talking Machines.* The Science Museum/HMSO, 1981.

Copeland, Peter. Record Dating Guides in *Historic Record Quarterly,* December 1988 and subsequent issues.

Field, Mike. *Restoring the Edison Gem Phonograph.* City of London Phonograph and Gramophone Society, 1986.

Frow, George. *The Edison Disc Phonographs.* Frow, 1982.

Frow, George. *The Edison Cylinder Phonograph Companion.* Baumbach (USA), 1994.

Hazelcorn, Howard. *The Columbia Spring-wound Cylinder Graphophone.* American Phonograph Monthly (USA), 1976.

Maken, Neil. *Hand-cranked Phonographs.* Promar Press (USA), 1993.

Proudfoot, Christopher. *Collecting Phonographs and Gramophones.* Studio Vista, 1980.

Reiss, Eric. *The Compleat Talking Machine.* Vestal Press (USA), 1986.

Rennie, Richard. *Care and Conservation of Talking Machines.* Papyrus Books (Australia), 1984.

Thomson, Alistair. *Phonographs and Gramophones Catalogue.* Royal Scottish Museum, 1977.

Welch, W. and Burt, L. *From Tinfoil to Stereo.* University of Florida Press (USA), 1994.

Various authors. *Phonographs and Gramophones Symposium.* Royal Scottish Museum, 1977.

Some of these books, and many others, are available through the City of London Phonograph and Gramophone Society, an international body which also publishes an invaluable bimonthly magazine, *Hillandale News*, and has produced reproduction spare parts for machines. Contact the Secretary, Ms Suzanne Lewis, 51 Brockhurst Road, Chesham, Buckinghamshire HP5 3JB.

PLACES TO VISIT

This list is not exhaustive. Many other museums with social history or technology displays include phonographs or gramophones, and more preserve them in storage. Intending visitors are advised to find out the opening times before making a special journey.

GREAT BRITAIN

Birmingham Museum of Science and Industry, Newhall Street, Birmingham, West Midlands B3 1RZ. Telephone: 0121 235 1661.

British Library National Sound Archive, 29 Exhibition Road, South Kensington, London SW7 2AS. Telephone: 0171 412 7440. Open every weekday.

Mechanical Music and Doll Collection, Church Road, Portfield, Chichester, West Sussex PO19 4HN. Telephone: 01243 785421.

The Museum of London, London Wall, London EC2Y 5HN. Telephone: 0171-600 3699. The collection is in storage but parties can be shown around by appointment.

The Musical Museum, 368 High Street, Brentford, Middlesex TW8 0BD. Telephone: 0181-560 8108.

Royal Museum of Scotland, Chambers Street, Edinburgh EH1 1JF. Telephone: 0131-225 7534. None of the collection is currently displayed. The stores may be accessible to researchers.

The Science Museum, Exhibition Road, South Kensington, London SW7 2DD. Telephone: 0171-938 8000. Little of the collection is currently on display, but researchers may visit the stores by appointment.

NETHERLANDS

Fonografisch Museum, Hoog Catharijne, Gildenkwartier 43, 3511 DB Utrecht.

SOUTH KOREA

Chamsori Gramophone and Audio Museum, 216-4 SongJung-dong, Kong Reung-city, Kangwon-Do.

UNITED STATES OF AMERICA

Edison Institute, Henry Ford Foundation, Dearborn, Michigan.

Edison National Historic Site, Main Street and Lakeside Avenue, West Orange, New Jersey 07052.

Edison Winter Home, Fort Myers, Florida.